AI Implement Innovation

Advanced Strategies for Successfully Adopting and Leveraging AI in Your Organization

Hamid Oudi

Disclaimer

The framework presented in this book reflects the professional opinion of the author based on their experience working in the sector for the past 15 years. Any potential value estimates on business revenue and profit from AI/Data Science integration are derived from case studies for similar clients. However, these estimates should not be viewed as promises or guarantees for future outcomes.

Use of Case Studies:
Due to confidentiality agreements and privacy concerns, the real-world case studies discussed in this book are based on anonymized scenarios. The businesses and characters, such as Tom, Sophia, and Olivia, are fictional and are used to represent general challenges and solutions in AI adoption. These examples explain the art of the possible in AI applications and are not drawn from specific, real-life clients. No confidential details have been disclosed.

Table of Contents

Introduction: The Power and Potential of AI for Every Business

The question for leaders today isn't whether AI should be adopted, but how quickly can it be integrated into their organizations to drive growth, enhance customer experiences, and increase operational efficiency.

This book is your guide to navigating the world of AI—from the initial stages of understanding what AI can do for your business, to successfully implementing it, scaling it, and managing AI projects effectively. Whether you're running a small business looking to automate routine tasks or leading a large enterprise striving to integrate AI across departments, this book is tailored for you. It will help you bridge the gap between the promise of AI and the practical steps required to make AI a game-changing reality in your organization.

AI is not just a trend. It's the key to unlocking faster decision-making, cost savings, personalized customer interactions, and smarter ways of working. But for many businesses, especially SMBs, the world of AI can seem overwhelming. Complex terminology, massive investment requirements, and technical barriers may prevent you from exploring AI's potential. However, the reality is that AI is now more accessible, affordable, and impactful than ever before, with tools and platforms designed to fit budgets of all sizes.

Through this book, we will demystify AI. We'll show you how to **implement AI in a manageable way**, **scale AI across your entire organization**, and **avoid common pitfalls** that often derail AI adoption. From understanding the technical requirements to managing cross-functional teams and driving AI projects forward, this book will provide you with **actionable steps** and **real-world case studies** to help you get started and scale AI effectively.

You'll also gain insight into the unique challenges and opportunities of scaling AI for small businesses—how you can use AI to compete with larger organizations without breaking the bank, and how AI can enable your team to work smarter, not harder.

Why Scaling AI Matters

The true power of AI lies in **scaling it**—from a small-scale pilot project to enterprise-wide integration. Many companies start AI initiatives in isolated pockets of their business, experimenting with AI in one department or function. While pilots often provide value, they are rarely enough to unlock AI's full potential. The key to AI's long-term success is scaling it to **every corner of your organization**, integrating AI tools and solutions across functions such as marketing, sales, customer service, and operations.

Scaling AI not only brings consistency, efficiency, and reliability, but it also maximizes return on investment (ROI). It allows organizations to standardize AI solutions across departments, making them more effective and reducing waste. Additionally, as AI solutions grow and evolve, they provide more value to your business by continually learning from data and improving processes.

Who This Book Is For

This book is for:

- **Business Leaders and Executives** looking to drive organizational transformation through AI.

- **Project Managers and AI Leads** tasked with overseeing the implementation, scaling, and management of AI projects.

- **Small Business Owners** who want to leverage AI to streamline operations, enhance customer engagement, and drive growth.

- **Anyone interested in AI** and how it can be harnessed to transform businesses at scale.

What You Will Learn

In the chapters that follow, you will explore:

- **The AI Adoption Journey**: How to prepare your organization for AI by aligning your strategy, people, and technology.

- **AI Project Management**: Best practices for managing AI projects, from planning and execution to delivery and optimization.

- **Scaling AI**: How to take a small AI pilot and turn it into an enterprise-wide transformation.

- **Real-World Applications**: Case studies of how businesses, both large and small, have successfully implemented and scaled AI.

- **Practical Tools and Templates**: AI project management templates, KPI trackers, and other tools to help you manage and measure AI initiatives.

By the end of this book, you will not only understand the fundamentals of AI, but also know how to **start small, scale effectively**, and avoid the common mistakes that often hinder successful AI adoption. Whether you're just getting started or are ready to scale AI across your organization, this guide will provide you with the tools, frameworks, and insights needed to succeed in the **age of AI**.

So, let's begin your journey to AI success. It's time to embrace AI—not just as a tool, but as a **strategic asset** that will drive your business forward.

Chapter 1: Why AI Matters and How It Can Transform Your Business

Despite the overwhelming potential AI holds, many businesses—especially small and medium-sized enterprises (SMBs)—remain hesitant to embrace this groundbreaking technology. The reasons for this reluctance vary from misconceptions about its complexity and cost to fears of being unable to implement it effectively.

The truth, however, is that AI is not just for the big players with deep pockets. It's accessible and highly relevant for businesses of all sizes. In fact, AI has the power to level the playing field, providing smaller businesses with the same opportunities to thrive as their larger counterparts. In this chapter, we will explore **why AI matters**, and how it can **transform your business**—whether you're just beginning to explore its potential or looking to scale it across your entire organization.

The Growing Need for AI in Business

Artificial Intelligence has quickly moved from the realm of science fiction to become an integral part of everyday business operations. The reality is that AI is already embedded in many of the tools that businesses use daily, even if they don't realize it. If you've ever received a personalized product recommendation on Amazon, used voice search on your smartphone, or interacted with a chatbot on a website, you've already experienced AI in action.

For large corporations like Amazon, AI has been the cornerstone of innovation. The company's AI-driven recommendation system analyses customer behaviour, purchase history, and browsing patterns to suggest products tailored specifically to everyone, helping drive sales and improve customer satisfaction. But this AI-powered revolution isn't limited to tech giants. Small businesses, too, are beginning to realize the immense value AI brings.

Take, for instance, a small clothing retailer that can use AI to predict fashion trends and adjust inventory levels accordingly. AI allows this small business to run more efficiently by automating tasks like inventory management and customer service, tasks that would have previously required a significant amount of time and labour. The AI-driven systems can analyse consumer data, track purchasing behaviours, and offer personalized recommendations, creating a more engaging shopping experience for customers without requiring a large team to run the operation.

The truth is, the potential of AI is not tied to the size of the business, but rather to how well businesses can harness the technology to their advantage. For small businesses, AI offers the ability to compete with larger organizations without needing a massive budget. AI allows these businesses to innovate in ways that weren't possible before and enables them to improve their efficiency, customer service, and decision-making processes.

How AI Can Transform Small Businesses

While many small business owners may believe that AI is something only accessible to large companies, the reality is far different. Today, **affordable, easy-to-use AI tools** are readily available, making it possible for even the smallest businesses to get started with AI without breaking the bank. These tools often require little to no technical expertise, allowing business owners to focus on the high-level strategy while AI handles the repetitive, time-consuming tasks.

For instance, consider a small café that uses an AI-powered system to manage inventory. The AI tool can track sales trends and predict which items are likely to sell out, automatically generating orders for fresh stock and preventing overstocking. This minimizes waste and reduces the amount of time staff need to spend on manual inventory checks. A few years ago, this level of operational insight might have been out of reach for such a small business, but today it's a reality that is achievable with minimal effort and cost.

AI can also help small businesses enhance customer experiences. Imagine a local boutique using an AI system to personalize the shopping experience for every customer. By analysing browsing behaviour and purchase history, AI can suggest new products that a customer might like, just as a larger store like Amazon does. For businesses with limited staff, this would have been a daunting task, but AI allows for **personalized experiences at scale**—a game-changer for small businesses looking to compete with much larger players.

But the impact of AI isn't just about improving operations or customer service. **AI can also empower small businesses to make smarter, data-driven decisions.** By analysing everything from customer behaviour to inventory levels, AI provides valuable insights that help business owners make more informed choices. Take a small restaurant that uses AI to analyse customer reviews and predict which menu items are likely to be popular in the coming months. Instead of relying on intuition, the business owner can make decisions based on hard data, leading to smarter business strategies and increased profitability.

AI at Scale: From Pilot to Enterprise-Wide Transformation

AI can start small—there's no need to dive into complex, enterprise-level solutions right away. For most businesses, including SMBs, the journey often begins with **pilot projects**— small, manageable experiments designed to test the waters and evaluate how AI can add value to specific aspects of the business. These pilot projects can range from AI-powered chatbots to inventory management systems. The goal is to prove that AI can drive value before committing to larger-scale implementation.

However, the true value of AI doesn't lie in small experiments—it lies in its ability to **scale across the organization**. As businesses begin to see the benefits of AI in isolated functions, they will want to expand its use across different departments and operations. For example, a small retail business that initially uses AI for inventory management may later apply AI to marketing, customer service, or sales strategies. As AI tools evolve and improve, scaling becomes a natural next step in the journey.

For large organizations, scaling AI means overcoming challenges such as fragmented data systems, siloed departments, and the need for robust infrastructure to handle the demands of enterprise-wide AI applications. But scaling AI is not just about expanding its footprint; it's about **integrating AI into the core of business**

strategy—ensuring that every decision made, every operation conducted, and every customer interaction is optimized with AI.

The concept of scaling AI also applies to small businesses. Scaling doesn't necessarily mean rolling out massive enterprise-wide solutions. Instead, small businesses can begin with one AI-driven tool or system and gradually integrate additional AI capabilities as the business grows. For example, a small business that starts with AI-powered marketing automation might later expand to include predictive analytics for customer behaviour or AI-driven inventory forecasting.

Why AI is Critical for Long-Term Business Success

AI is not just a short-term fix or a passing trend. **It's the future of business**, and it's already changing the way companies operate across the globe. The businesses that are adopting AI today are not just solving immediate problems—they are positioning themselves for future growth and success. As market dynamics evolve and customer expectations shift, businesses that fail to embrace AI will be left behind. Early AI adopters are already gaining an edge, creating **smarter**, **faster**, and more **personalized** customer experiences that drive competitive advantage.

The need for AI is about more than just improving existing processes. It's about ensuring that your business is **future-proof**— able to adapt quickly to new market demands, shifts in consumer behaviour, and emerging trends. AI helps businesses remain agile, enabling them to **anticipate trends**, **respond faster to customer needs**, and **optimize operations** across departments. In today's fast-paced world, the companies that fail to leverage AI risk being left behind as more agile, AI-enabled competitors race ahead.

By adopting AI now, businesses can create a foundation for **long-term sustainability**. Whether it's enhancing efficiency, improving decision-making, or boosting customer satisfaction, AI is a tool that will continue to evolve and offer even greater benefits in the years to come. The longer a business waits to adopt AI, the harder it will be to catch up to competitors who have already embraced the technology and scaled it across their operations.

The Leadership Role in AI Adoption

For AI to succeed in any organization, it needs the backing of strong leadership. AI adoption isn't just about installing new technology—it's about **leading a cultural shift** within the business. AI transforms not just operations, but the way employees work, how teams collaborate, and how decisions are made. As a business leader, your role is to guide your organization through this transformation.

Leaders must ensure that AI is aligned with the **business goals** of the organization, building a clear roadmap for how AI will drive success. They must also foster a culture that embraces change, innovation, and continuous learning—qualities that are critical for AI adoption. Leaders must communicate the value of AI, ensuring that employees see it as a tool to enhance their roles, not replace them. This helps build trust in the technology and minimizes resistance.

AI adoption is not without its challenges, but with the right leadership and vision, businesses can successfully integrate AI into their operations and scale it over time.

The future of business is here, and AI is at the forefront of this transformation. Whether you're running a small business looking to compete with larger players or leading a large organization in need of greater efficiency, AI has the potential to **revolutionize** the way you operate. The time to adopt AI is now. Whether you start small or scale rapidly, the opportunities are endless. This book will guide you on your journey to successfully implement, scale, and manage AI in your business, giving you the tools you need to thrive in the AI-driven future.

The question is no longer if AI will transform your business, but **how soon can you begin?**

Chapter 2: Laying the Foundation for AI Success in Your Business

Before jumping into the deep end, it's crucial to lay a solid foundation that ensures your business is prepared to implement AI effectively and scale it successfully over time.

In this chapter, we will explore how to assess your organization's **readiness for AI**, the importance of building the right **infrastructure**, and how to create a culture that embraces innovation and change. We will walk through the essential steps of getting your business ready for AI adoption, focusing on the elements that are often overlooked but are critical to ensuring that AI is integrated smoothly into your organization's processes.

Understanding AI Readiness: Is Your Business Ready?

Before embarking on the AI journey, the first step is to assess whether your business is truly ready for AI adoption. It's easy to get excited about the possibilities that AI can bring, but without the necessary groundwork, you may encounter roadblocks down the line. Ensuring that your business is ready is key to avoiding wasted time and resources.

AI readiness is a multi-faceted concept, and it involves several critical components. The most important of these include **data**, **technology infrastructure**, and **skills**. Each of these elements must be carefully evaluated and aligned before implementing AI at any scale.

Data Readiness

Data is the lifeblood of any AI system. AI systems rely on data to function—without high-quality, well-organized data, even the most advanced AI algorithms will struggle to provide meaningful results. Assessing your data readiness begins with an honest evaluation of your existing data sources.

For many businesses, especially small ones, **data quality** is a major challenge. Often, businesses don't have the robust data systems in place that larger organizations do. Data may be stored in disparate systems, incomplete, or even outright inaccessible. The challenge, therefore, lies in **data consolidation**—integrating data from various sources and making it readily available for AI systems.

Data readiness also includes the **ethical use of data**. As your organization starts integrating AI, it's important to ensure that your data collection methods are transparent and ethical. For example, businesses must ensure they have proper consent from customers for collecting data and using it to drive AI models. Additionally, addressing privacy concerns and avoiding data biases are vital considerations that need to be woven into your AI adoption process.

To get started, businesses must first assess the availability, cleanliness, and accessibility of their data. Begin by ensuring that the data is stored in a **structured format** that can easily be fed into AI systems, and that there are systems in place for data

governance. This will lay the groundwork for AI-driven systems that can provide actionable insights.

Technology Infrastructure

Next, AI demands a specific level of technology infrastructure to work effectively. You must ensure that your existing infrastructure can handle the computational power required to run AI models. This doesn't necessarily mean that you need to make a massive investment in new hardware, but you do need to ensure that your **cloud services**, **data storage**, and **network security** systems can support the tools and platforms you plan to implement.

For SMBs, the solution often lies in **cloud-based AI services**. These services offer a scalable and cost-effective way to access the computational power needed to run sophisticated AI algorithms. They also provide access to **AI tools** that are ready to use, such as machine learning models, natural language processing systems, and data visualization platforms, without the need for an in-house data science team to build these models from scratch.

Cloud services like Amazon Web Services (AWS), Microsoft Azure, and Google Cloud are already equipped with AI platforms designed to help businesses integrate AI at scale, allowing businesses to access these powerful tools without the need to own expensive hardware or maintain complex infrastructure. These cloud-based solutions allow SMBs to pay only for what they use, making it a much more affordable option for businesses with limited resources.

In addition to the cloud, businesses need to ensure their **network security** is up to par. As AI systems rely on vast amounts of data, ensuring that sensitive customer information is protected from breaches is a top priority. Establishing **security protocols** and ensuring compliance with relevant regulations (such as GDPR for companies operating in Europe) is essential before deploying any AI tools.

Skills and Talent

AI implementation also demands a workforce that is **equipped with the right skills**. This doesn't mean every employee needs to be an AI expert, but there needs to be a clear strategy for building or acquiring the necessary skills. Having **data scientists, AI specialists**, or **technical consultants** is ideal for businesses that want to create and optimize AI models in-house. However, many businesses, especially SMBs, choose to partner with AI service providers or use pre-built tools to bypass the need for heavy technical expertise.

Even though AI tools have become more user-friendly, **data literacy** within your team is crucial. Ensuring your employees understand the importance of data, how it can be leveraged, and how AI works will help in **building a culture of AI adoption**. This is especially important for business leaders and managers who may need to align AI initiatives with organizational strategy and goals.

For businesses that don't yet have AI skills on board, consider **training programs** and **external partnerships**. There are plenty of educational resources available for both beginners and advanced practitioners, and many online platforms offer tailored AI courses designed for professionals. By investing in skill development, businesses can ensure they have the internal expertise to support their AI initiatives, either through upskilling existing staff or hiring new talent.

Building a Culture for AI: Change Management and Innovation

AI adoption is not just about technology—it's about people. While technical infrastructure and data readiness are essential, the most important ingredient for AI success is creating a culture that is **open to innovation** and willing to embrace change. The **cultural shift** required for AI adoption can be one of the most challenging aspects of the process, especially if employees are resistant or fear that AI will replace their roles.

Business leaders need to actively foster a culture of **collaboration** and **transparency** where AI is seen as a **tool to augment human capability**, not a threat. Employees must understand how AI will support their work, make processes more efficient, and free them from mundane tasks. Emphasizing AI as a **collaborative partner** rather than a job replacement is crucial for building trust and engagement.

Leaders also need to ensure that AI is **aligned with business goals**. This means that AI initiatives should be carefully planned and integrated into the broader business strategy. It's easy to get excited about the possibilities AI offers, but it's important to **set clear objectives** and measure success. Leaders should think about what they want to achieve with AI—whether it's improving customer service, optimizing logistics, or increasing sales—and focus on aligning AI solutions with those goals.

At the same time, change management practices must be in place to help teams navigate through the transition. Communication is key, and business leaders must provide consistent updates on AI initiatives, explaining the benefits and addressing any concerns employees may have. Providing **training and support** during the implementation phase can help reduce anxiety and ensure smoother transitions as AI tools are adopted across different teams.

As businesses scale AI across departments, collaboration between teams becomes essential. AI should not be a siloed function but integrated across various business units, from marketing to operations to customer service. **Cross-functional collaboration** allows for the sharing of insights, encourages the exchange of ideas, and ensures that AI initiatives are well-supported throughout the organization.

Aligning AI with Business Strategy

Before implementing AI, it's crucial to ensure that AI initiatives are aligned with the **overall business strategy**. This means understanding your organization's core objectives, identifying areas where AI can provide the most value, and designing AI solutions that directly contribute to achieving those objectives.

For example, a retail business looking to improve customer service may focus on AI-powered chatbots that can handle customer inquiries 24/7. A manufacturing company, on the other hand, may prioritize predictive maintenance to reduce downtime and extend the life of equipment. These AI initiatives must be **purpose-**

driven and aligned with the company's mission, vision, and long-term goals.

Building a **roadmap** for AI adoption that aligns with business goals ensures that the technology is deployed strategically, and that the return on investment is maximized. Business leaders must prioritize AI projects that will deliver the most significant impact first and scale them gradually, rather than trying to tackle too many things at once.

One of the most effective ways to ensure alignment is by establishing **clear success metrics** for AI projects. This could be in the form of increased revenue, reduced costs, improved customer satisfaction, or enhanced operational efficiency. Whatever the goals, measuring success ensures that businesses stay on track and can **adjust strategies** if necessary.

The Road Ahead: What's Next for AI Implementation

Having laid the foundation for AI, the next step is to **start implementing** the technology in a way that aligns with your business objectives and scales effectively over time. From data readiness and technology infrastructure to cultural transformation and business strategy alignment, every step you take now will shape your future success with AI.

In the next chapters, we will discuss practical steps for **getting started with AI, overcoming common obstacles,** and **scaling AI solutions across your business**. By following the guidance in this chapter and taking the time to build a strong AI foundation, your business will be well-equipped to navigate the complexities of AI adoption and drive long-term success.

Chapter 3: Building Your AI Strategy: From Pilot to Scalable Success

As businesses begin their journey into the world of AI, one of the most important tasks is to develop a clear and effective AI strategy. Implementing AI isn't as simple as just adopting a new technology—it's about rethinking how the organization operates, aligns its goals, and manages its resources. To maximize the potential of AI, businesses must build a strategy that is not only focused on quick wins but also on long-term scalability, adaptability, and alignment with broader business objectives.

In this chapter, we will dive deep into how to build an AI strategy that enables businesses to transition from small-scale pilot projects to enterprise-wide AI initiatives. The process involves several critical steps: **identifying the right AI opportunities**, **setting measurable goals**, **managing cross-functional collaboration**, **aligning AI initiatives with business objectives**, and **creating the necessary infrastructure** for growth. By understanding these elements and integrating them into your organization's strategic planning, you can ensure that your AI projects deliver maximum value, scale successfully, and contribute to the overall success of the business.

Identifying the Right AI Opportunities: Where to Start

The first step in building an effective AI strategy is identifying the right opportunities. Not every business function or process is ripe for AI, and not every problem is best solved by artificial intelligence. To maximize the impact of AI, it's essential to focus on areas where AI can make a tangible difference. This requires understanding both the limitations and the potential of AI and then mapping it to the areas of your business that will benefit most from automation, insights, or optimization.

For many businesses, the most promising AI opportunities lie in automating **repetitive tasks**, improving **decision-making** through data analysis, and enhancing **customer engagement** through personalized services. Take, for example, a small e-commerce store. AI could be used to automate inventory management, predict customer demand, or personalize product recommendations based on browsing and purchase history. These are areas where AI can bring immediate value, freeing up time and resources while improving business outcomes.

AI can also play a crucial role in improving **customer experience**. Many businesses have adopted AI-driven chatbots, which can handle customer inquiries, process orders, and offer personalized product suggestions, all without human intervention. For larger organizations, the opportunities are even more expansive—AI can optimize supply chains, manage HR processes, predict sales trends, and even support strategic decision-making by analysing data at scale.

When considering where to apply AI, it's also important to **start small**. Many businesses begin with a specific problem or use case, such as automating a customer service function, and then expand the use of AI as they gain confidence and experience. This "start small and scale" approach ensures that businesses can measure the success of their initial AI projects and expand them gradually, with minimal risk.

Setting Clear, Measurable Goals for AI Initiatives

One of the most critical aspects of any AI strategy is setting clear, measurable goals. Without clearly defined objectives, it's impossible to gauge the success of AI projects, manage expectations, or align AI initiatives with broader business goals. The challenge, however, is ensuring that these goals are realistic and achievable. AI is a powerful tool, but it requires careful planning and execution to deliver real value.

Start by identifying **key business problems** that AI can solve. Are you looking to increase operational efficiency? Improve customer service? Boost sales? Enhance marketing targeting? Whatever the goals are, they should be **specific, measurable, attainable, relevant, and time-bound** (SMART). This approach ensures that AI initiatives are focused on business outcomes that matter, rather than on the technology itself.

For instance, if you're using AI to automate customer service, a clear goal might be to **reduce response times by 50%** or **increase customer satisfaction by 20%** within the next six months. If you're using AI to optimize inventory management, a goal might be to **reduce stockouts by 30%** or **improve inventory turnover by 15%**. By setting measurable goals like these, businesses can track their progress and ensure that their AI initiatives are delivering tangible benefits.

Moreover, businesses should define **success metrics** for each AI initiative. These metrics can include operational improvements, cost savings, revenue growth, customer retention rates, or any other relevant business KPI. Regularly measuring and reporting on these metrics will help you assess whether AI is achieving the desired results, and if not, what adjustments need to be made.

Managing Cross-Functional Collaboration for AI Projects

AI projects typically require a **cross-functional approach**, as they involve a wide range of stakeholders and expertise from different areas of the business. For example, implementing an AI-driven customer service tool might require input from IT, customer support, marketing, and sales teams, each of which brings its own perspective and expertise to the table. One of the key challenges in building an AI strategy is ensuring that these departments work together seamlessly to deliver successful outcomes.

The success of any AI project depends heavily on **clear communication**, **shared objectives**, and effective **collaboration**. It's crucial to ensure that everyone involved in the project understands not only the technical aspects of AI but also how AI can drive value for the business. Each team needs to see AI as an enabler of their work rather than a disruptive force that will replace their roles.

One of the first steps in building an AI strategy is to **establish a project team** with diverse expertise. This could include **data scientists**, **engineers**, **business analysts**, and **subject-matter experts** from the relevant business areas. The team should be tasked with defining the scope of the AI initiative, outlining the desired outcomes, and ensuring that AI solutions are aligned with business objectives.

Additionally, businesses must ensure **continuous communication** throughout the AI project lifecycle. Regular meetings and updates will keep all stakeholders aligned and help identify and address any issues before they become roadblocks. It's also important to ensure that leadership is engaged in the process, as AI initiatives often require significant investment and strategic oversight.

Aligning AI Initiatives with Broader Business Objectives

AI can offer a wealth of benefits to businesses, but to achieve maximum impact, AI initiatives must be closely aligned with the organization's broader strategic goals. AI should never be viewed as a standalone technology but as an integral part of the overall business strategy. Whether the goal is to enhance customer satisfaction, optimize operations, or drive innovation, AI initiatives must support and reinforce the company's mission and vision.

For example, a company focused on **improving customer experiences** could use AI to personalize interactions with customers, predicting their needs and offering tailored recommendations. A business looking to **increase efficiency** could use AI to automate processes like invoicing, procurement, or supply chain management. No matter the focus, AI projects must be tied to clear business objectives to ensure that the technology delivers the desired outcomes.

Building an AI strategy that aligns with business goals requires **clear communication between departments**. Business leaders must work with technical teams to ensure that AI solutions are not only feasible from a technical standpoint but also meet the needs of the business. A collaborative, cross-functional approach ensures that AI projects are aligned with the company's strategic priorities, and that the business is getting the most value out of its AI investments.

Creating the Necessary Infrastructure for AI Growth

While building a strategy is crucial, so is preparing the **infrastructure** that will support the growth of AI initiatives. AI requires powerful technology infrastructure to process large amounts of data, run complex algorithms, and store the insights generated. For businesses that are just beginning to explore AI, this doesn't mean making huge investments in new hardware or proprietary systems. Instead, it involves ensuring that the business has the **scalable** and **secure infrastructure** needed to support AI applications.

For small businesses, **cloud computing** offers an affordable, scalable solution. Cloud-based AI tools and services provide businesses with access to advanced AI capabilities without the need to invest in expensive hardware or hire a large technical team. Cloud platforms like Google Cloud, Amazon Web Services (AWS), and Microsoft Azure provide a wide range of **AI tools**, from machine learning models to natural language processing tools, that businesses can integrate into their operations without the complexity of building solutions from scratch.

Additionally, businesses must ensure that their **data infrastructure** can support AI initiatives. This includes ensuring that data is stored in a secure, accessible manner, that data privacy regulations are adhered to, and that data is clean and well-organized. Without a solid data foundation, AI systems cannot function effectively. Data governance, quality control, and security protocols must be implemented to ensure that the data used for AI is both reliable and compliant.

As AI initiatives scale, businesses must continue to invest in infrastructure that can handle growing volumes of data and more complex AI models. Ensuring that the necessary **technology platforms** and **cloud services** are in place will allow businesses to expand their AI capabilities as their needs evolve.

Scaling AI: From Small Wins to Long-Term Transformation

Once the foundation is laid and AI initiatives have begun to show success, the next step is scaling. Scaling AI is about expanding from small, pilot projects to enterprise-wide integration. It requires the right infrastructure, the right people, and the right processes to ensure that AI can deliver consistent value across the organization.

Scaling AI also means integrating AI into the **company culture**. For AI to be truly successful at scale, it needs to be embraced by employees across all departments. This means that leadership must continue to foster a culture of **innovation**, **collaboration**, and **continuous improvement**. Employees must be trained, supported, and encouraged to embrace AI, using it as a tool to enhance their work, not as a technology that will replace them.

As you scale AI, it's also essential to measure and evaluate progress regularly. Ensuring that AI initiatives remain aligned with business goals, and adjusting strategies based on feedback and data, is key to long-term success.

Building a comprehensive AI strategy requires careful planning, clear goals, strong collaboration, and an infrastructure capable of supporting AI's growth. By taking a structured, strategic approach to AI, businesses can maximize the value of AI technologies, drive innovation, and achieve long-term success. The next step in your AI journey will involve putting these strategies into action and scaling AI solutions across your organization for sustained growth.

Chapter 4: Overcoming Challenges in AI Adoption and Scaling

As businesses embark on their AI journey, they must be prepared to face the various obstacles that can arise, from technical issues to cultural resistance. These challenges can vary depending on the size of the organization, its existing infrastructure, and its level of familiarity with AI. However, understanding and preparing for these obstacles is crucial for the success of any AI initiative.

In this chapter, we will explore the common challenges businesses face when adopting and scaling AI, and how to effectively navigate these hurdles. By addressing issues such as data quality, technical debt, resistance to change, and the need for skilled talent, businesses can ensure that their AI projects are successful, scalable, and sustainable.

Data Quality and Availability: The Foundation of AI

Data is at the core of AI systems. Without good data, AI can't function effectively, no matter how advanced the algorithm or the model. This is one of the first and most significant challenges businesses face when implementing AI—**data quality**. AI systems are only as good as the data they are trained on, and if the data is incomplete, inconsistent, or inaccurate, the resulting insights and predictions can be flawed.

Many businesses struggle with **data silos**—where data is scattered across different departments or systems and is difficult to access and integrate. For instance, sales data might be stored in one system, customer service data in another, and inventory data in yet another, making it impossible to get a comprehensive view of the business. These silos not only hinder AI initiatives but also lead to inefficiencies and missed opportunities.

To overcome this challenge, businesses must prioritize **data governance** and **data integration**. This means ensuring that data is properly organized, stored securely, and made accessible across the entire organization. It's crucial to establish processes for **data cleaning**, so that any discrepancies in the data are identified and addressed before they can impact AI models.

Moreover, businesses must ensure that they are collecting **the right data**. This includes data that is not only relevant to AI models but also representative of the problem the business is trying to solve. Collecting the right type of data involves understanding the underlying business problem and ensuring that data is collected in a structured, consistent way that AI systems can process.

Finally, businesses must pay attention to **data privacy** and **compliance** issues. AI systems often rely on vast amounts of customer data, and mishandling this data can lead to privacy violations, legal issues, and reputational damage. Adhering to data protection regulations, such as the General Data Protection Regulation (GDPR) or the California Consumer Privacy Act (CCPA), is essential to maintaining customer trust and avoiding costly fines.

Overcoming Technical Debt and Integration Issues

AI adoption often involves integrating new technologies into existing systems. However, many businesses are burdened with what's known as **technical debt**—the cost of maintaining and updating outdated systems and software. As businesses introduce new AI tools and platforms, they may face challenges integrating these technologies with legacy systems, which were not designed with AI in mind.

One common issue is that legacy systems are often **disconnected** or **incompatible** with modern AI tools. For example, a company may have a legacy inventory management system that isn't designed to handle the data streams required for AI-based predictions. Similarly, customer service platforms may not have the infrastructure to support AI chatbots or virtual assistants.

To address these integration challenges, businesses need to invest in **upgrading their technology infrastructure**. This could mean modernizing legacy systems to make them more compatible with AI or migrating to cloud-based platforms that are designed for scalability and flexibility. Cloud services like Amazon Web Services (AWS), Microsoft Azure, and Google Cloud provide a wide range of tools and solutions that integrate easily with existing business systems, helping to reduce the complexity of the integration process.

Another way to reduce technical debt is by adopting **modular AI solutions** that can be integrated with existing systems without requiring a complete overhaul. For example, businesses can use

AI-as-a-service platforms, where the AI capabilities are delivered through the cloud and are relatively easy to integrate into existing systems. These solutions are more cost-effective and less disruptive than building custom AI tools from scratch, making them a great option for businesses looking to scale AI quickly without overhauling their entire technology stack.

Addressing Cultural Resistance: Engaging Employees and Stakeholders

While the technical challenges of AI adoption are significant, **cultural resistance** can often be the hardest barrier to overcome. AI represents a fundamental shift in the way businesses operate, and as such, employees may fear that automation and AI will replace their roles, leaving them out of work. In some cases, employees may simply be sceptical about the value AI can bring to their jobs or the business.

This resistance is not limited to the workforce; it can also come from management or other stakeholders who may not fully understand the value of AI or who may be hesitant to invest in what they perceive as an uncertain technology. This fear of change and lack of understanding can slow down AI adoption and hinder the overall success of AI projects.

To overcome this resistance, businesses must focus on **change management** and **clear communication**. Leaders must educate employees about the benefits of AI, both for the business and for their own roles. AI should be framed as a tool that **augments human capabilities**, not as a replacement for jobs. By showing how AI can take over repetitive, mundane tasks, employees can focus on more strategic and creative aspects of their work.

Leadership should also involve employees in the AI adoption process from the very beginning. This could involve gathering feedback from employees on where they see AI having the most impact, as well as involving them in the development and testing of AI tools. When employees feel that they are part of the process, they are more likely to embrace AI and see it as a positive change rather than a threat.

Furthermore, businesses should provide **training and reskilling opportunities** to ensure that employees are equipped with the skills necessary to work alongside AI systems. This not only helps employees adapt to new technologies but also increases overall job satisfaction and engagement. It's essential to make AI adoption an **inclusive process**, where all employees can learn and grow alongside the technology.

Building the Right Talent and Skills for AI

Another significant challenge in AI adoption is the **shortage of skilled talent**. AI requires a combination of technical skills, such as machine learning and data science, as well as domain knowledge to ensure that AI systems are properly applied to the business problem at hand. However, finding the right talent—especially for SMBs—is often a difficult and expensive process.

To address this challenge, businesses must focus on **talent development** and **collaboration**. For smaller organizations that may not be able to hire a full team of data scientists or AI specialists, partnering with external consultants or AI service providers can help fill the gap. Many cloud-based AI platforms also offer **pre-trained models** that don't require in-depth technical knowledge to use, making them accessible to businesses without specialized expertise.

However, it's also important to **upskill existing employees**. Many businesses already have employees with strong analytical skills, but they may not be familiar with AI or machine learning. By offering **training programs**, workshops, and certification courses, businesses can build their internal talent pool and ensure that employees are ready to work with AI systems. There are many online platforms that provide affordable AI training, such as Coursera, edX, and Udacity, which offer specialized courses in AI, machine learning, and data science.

Investing in talent development not only helps overcome the talent shortage but also contributes to a culture of continuous learning and innovation. As AI continues to evolve, businesses must ensure that their teams have the necessary skills to adapt to new technologies and stay ahead of the competition.

Ensuring Scalability: Planning for the Future

Once AI systems are up and running, businesses must focus on **scalability**. It's easy to implement a small AI project but ensuring that AI initiatives can scale across the organization is a more complex challenge. Scaling AI requires significant planning, investment in infrastructure, and a focus on long-term goals.

One of the key aspects of scaling AI is ensuring that the **data infrastructure** can handle growing volumes of data. As AI systems process more data and make more complex predictions, businesses need to invest in robust data management systems that can store and process large datasets in real-time. Cloud platforms can play a key role in scaling AI, as they offer the flexibility to expand computing power as needed.

Additionally, businesses must ensure that their **AI models are adaptable**. AI solutions are not static—they need to be continuously updated and refined as new data comes in. As AI models scale, businesses must invest in **monitoring and optimization** to ensure that the systems continue to provide accurate and relevant insights.

Finally, businesses must ensure that AI projects are **aligned with evolving business goals**. As the organization grows and new challenges emerge, the role of AI may change. By building flexibility into the AI strategy and ensuring that AI initiatives are aligned with the company's long-term vision, businesses can maximize the long-term benefits of AI.

Overcoming AI Adoption Challenges: The Road to Success

AI adoption is undoubtedly challenging, but it also presents incredible opportunities. By addressing the common challenges that businesses face—from data quality and technical debt to cultural resistance and talent shortages—organizations can ensure that their AI initiatives are successful and scalable. The key is to focus on the long-term value of AI, integrate it into the broader business strategy, and engage all stakeholders in the process. With careful planning, collaboration, and commitment, businesses can overcome these challenges and harness the transformative power of AI to drive growth, innovation, and success.

Chapter 5: Scaling AI Across the Organization: From Pilot to Full Integration

As businesses move forward with AI initiatives, one of the most important steps in the journey is scaling AI across the entire organization. While starting with pilot projects is an effective way to test AI capabilities, true success comes when AI solutions are fully integrated into core business processes and applied across multiple departments. This transformation can bring substantial benefits, but it also requires careful planning, the right resources, and a strategic vision. In this chapter, we will explore how businesses can move from small-scale AI projects to large-scale AI transformations, ensuring that AI delivers value across the entire organization.

The Importance of Scaling AI

Scaling AI goes far beyond implementing a single AI application or solution in one department. For AI to truly transform a business, it must be integrated across various functions and processes. Scaling AI offers the opportunity to achieve **consistency**, **efficiency**, and **improved decision-making** throughout the entire organization. However, it is also a process that requires careful thought, alignment with business objectives, and strong leadership.

When scaling AI, businesses can expect to see significant improvements in operational efficiency, customer experience, and revenue growth. For instance, a large retailer might begin with a recommendation engine on their e-commerce platform. As AI is scaled, it could be expanded to their brick-and-mortar stores for in-person product recommendations, integrated into their supply chain for demand forecasting, and utilized across their marketing teams for personalized customer outreach. This level of scale creates a comprehensive, data-driven ecosystem that enhances both the front-end customer experience and back-end operations.

Moreover, scaling AI allows businesses to **standardize solutions** across departments. This consistency reduces redundancies, improves collaboration between teams, and ensures that all parts of the business are working with the most up-to-date and accurate data. For organizations looking to compete in an AI-driven world, scaling AI is no longer optional—it is essential to maintaining competitiveness, ensuring sustainable growth, and providing superior customer value.

Key Steps for Scaling AI Successfully

1. Align AI with Organizational Goals

The first step in scaling AI is ensuring that it is aligned with the overall strategic goals of the business. Scaling AI across the organization is not just about applying technology everywhere; it's about ensuring that AI initiatives help meet broader business objectives such as increasing operational efficiency, enhancing customer satisfaction, or improving product development. AI solutions must be integrated into the organization's strategic vision to maximize their impact.

For example, if a company's goal is to enhance its customer service experience, AI-powered chatbots could be scaled across multiple channels (website, mobile app, social media) to provide consistent, round-the-clock support. Similarly, if operational efficiency is a primary goal, AI could be applied to automate processes such as inventory management, order fulfilment, and financial reporting.

By aligning AI initiatives with business objectives, leaders can ensure that AI delivers measurable value and supports long-term success. This alignment helps avoid unnecessary complexity and ensures that AI remains focused on solving real business problems, rather than being used for the sake of technology itself.

2. Build a Scalable Data Infrastructure

As businesses begin to scale their AI initiatives, they must ensure that their **data infrastructure** can support larger volumes of data and more complex AI models. In the early stages of AI adoption, businesses may have used small, siloed datasets or cloud-based AI tools that could be easily scaled up. However, as AI is scaled across the organization, businesses need to build robust data management systems that can handle the demands of large-scale AI.

A scalable data infrastructure means implementing systems that can store, manage, and process data from multiple sources in real-time. This could involve using **data lakes**, **data warehouses**, or advanced **cloud-based platforms** that support big data analytics. Businesses also need to ensure that they have the necessary systems in place to handle **data security**, **privacy regulations**, and **compliance** issues.

Building the right data infrastructure is critical to ensuring that AI can be scaled seamlessly. As more departments begin using AI, businesses must ensure that all the data flowing into the system is clean, consistent, and easily accessible for AI models. Investing in scalable cloud platforms and data integration tools will help ensure that the organization can handle growing data volumes and make real-time decisions based on up-to-date information.

3. Ensure Cross-Functional Collaboration

Scaling AI across an organization requires close collaboration between technical and non-technical teams. Unlike traditional IT projects, AI initiatives often require input from diverse teams, including data scientists, IT professionals, business analysts, and subject matter experts from various departments. Cross-functional collaboration ensures that AI solutions are designed with both technical feasibility and business relevance in mind.

One of the common mistakes businesses make when scaling AI is treating it as a **technical project** rather than a **strategic business initiative**. This can lead to siloed efforts, misaligned objectives, and a lack of buy-in from key stakeholders. To avoid this, businesses should establish **cross-functional teams** with representatives from different departments who are responsible for overseeing AI implementation and scaling.

These cross-functional teams can help break down barriers between departments, ensuring that AI is integrated into various business functions, from marketing and sales to customer service and operations. Collaboration ensures that AI solutions are aligned with the specific needs of each department while ensuring consistency across the organization.

4. Focus on Change Management and Employee Engagement

AI adoption at scale requires a significant shift in organizational culture, and this change must be carefully managed. One of the biggest obstacles to scaling AI is **employee resistance**. Many employees fear that AI will replace their jobs, leading to anxiety and reluctance to adopt new technologies. To overcome this, businesses must invest in **change management** strategies that promote understanding, transparency, and employee engagement.

Clear communication is essential. Leadership must actively engage employees at all levels, explaining the value of AI and how it will support their work rather than replace it. Business leaders should emphasize how AI can handle repetitive, mundane tasks, allowing employees to focus on higher-value activities that require creativity and human judgment.

Additionally, businesses should provide ongoing **training and support** to help employees adapt to new AI systems. Upskilling programs can help employees gain the technical skills they need to work alongside AI, enabling them to take full advantage of the new technology. By fostering a culture of innovation and learning, businesses can ensure that employees are onboard with AI adoption and feel empowered to use AI tools in their day-to-day work.

5. Continuously Monitor and Optimize AI Solutions

AI systems, especially those scaled across an organization, are not static—they must be **monitored** and **optimized** over time to ensure they continue to deliver value. As businesses scale AI, the complexity of the systems increases, and so does the need for continuous optimization.

This requires implementing **monitoring systems** that track the performance of AI models and flag any issues. Regular audits can help ensure that AI systems are still aligned with business goals, that they are functioning as expected, and that they are free from biases or errors. Optimization may involve retraining AI models with new data, adjusting parameters, or integrating new AI technologies as they become available.

Businesses should also gather feedback from employees who are using AI tools daily. This feedback can be invaluable for identifying areas for improvement and ensuring that AI solutions are meeting the needs of the business. With continuous monitoring and optimization, businesses can ensure that AI remains an asset and evolves in tandem with the organization's growth.

The Road Ahead: Scaling AI for Long-Term Success

Scaling AI is a complex but necessary process for businesses that want to remain competitive and drive sustainable growth. It requires careful planning, alignment with business goals, strong leadership, and a focus on both the technical and cultural aspects of AI adoption. By following the steps outlined in this chapter, businesses can move from small pilot projects to full-scale AI transformations that deliver measurable value across the entire organization.

The key to successful AI scaling lies in **adaptability**. AI technologies are rapidly evolving, and businesses must be prepared to continuously refine and optimize their AI systems as new capabilities emerge. Scaling AI is not a one-time project; it's an ongoing process of evolution, innovation, and learning.

As businesses continue to scale AI, they must focus on fostering a culture of **continuous improvement**. By integrating AI into all aspects of the organization, from customer service and marketing to operations and supply chain management, businesses can create a unified, data-driven ecosystem that enhances both internal processes and the customer experience. The true power of AI lies in its ability to scale and evolve, driving long-term success and creating a competitive advantage in an increasingly AI-driven world.

The journey to AI scalability is both challenging and rewarding, but with the right strategies in place, businesses can unlock the full potential of AI and build a foundation for **sustained growth and innovation**. The future of business is AI-driven, and those who successfully scale AI will be well-positioned to lead in the marketplace.

Chapter 6: AI-Driven Innovation: Leveraging AI for Competitive Advantage

For businesses looking to thrive in an AI-driven world, embracing **AI-driven innovation** is essential for staying ahead of the competition and positioning the organization for long-term success.

In this chapter, we will explore how businesses can leverage AI to fuel innovation, disrupt traditional industries, and differentiate themselves in the marketplace. We will delve into the different ways AI can be used to **create new revenue streams**, **enhance product development**, and **optimize customer experiences**. By understanding the various applications of AI-driven innovation, organizations can harness its full potential to gain a **competitive edge** and future-proof their business.

The Role of AI in Driving Business Model Innovation

One of the most exciting opportunities AI presents is the ability to **reimagine business models**. AI is not just about automating existing processes; it has the potential to transform the way a company operates and delivers value to customers. By integrating AI into the business model, organizations can create entirely new ways of generating revenue, engaging customers, and delivering products and services.

For example, traditional industries like retail, banking, and healthcare are being disrupted by AI-driven innovations. Take the example of **retail**—AI-powered recommendation engines, personalized shopping experiences, and real-time inventory management are transforming how retailers engage with customers and manage operations. Similarly, in **banking**, AI is used to detect fraud, provide personalized financial advice, and optimize investment strategies. In **healthcare**, AI-driven diagnostics and predictive analytics are enabling better patient outcomes and more efficient care delivery.

AI-driven business models can take many forms. For example:

- **AI as a Service (AIaaS)**: Businesses can offer AI capabilities through cloud-based platforms, allowing other organizations to integrate advanced AI tools without needing extensive infrastructure or in-house expertise. This approach democratizes access to AI and opens new revenue streams for businesses providing the service.

- **Subscription-Based AI Models**: Companies can offer AI-powered solutions on a subscription basis, providing customers with ongoing access to AI-driven tools and services. This model creates a recurring revenue stream while allowing businesses to continuously improve their AI offerings.

- **Data Monetization**: As businesses collect more data through AI systems, they can create new ways to monetize that data. For example, selling anonymized customer insights or offering data-driven reports can create a new source of income.

By rethinking traditional business models and leveraging AI as a core component, companies can **disrupt industries**, **open new markets**, and establish themselves as leaders in innovation.

Enhancing Product and Service Innovation with AI

AI doesn't just help businesses improve existing products—it can be a **catalyst for entirely new product and service innovations**. By using AI to gain deeper insights into customer needs, market trends, and product performance, companies can develop more innovative solutions that align with the evolving demands of the market.

Consider the impact of AI on product design and development. Traditionally, product development cycles were long and based on assumptions about customer preferences. Today, AI enables businesses to **predict** and **analyse** customer preferences in real-time, leading to products that are more closely aligned with customer needs. For example, AI can analyse purchasing behaviour, social media activity, and market trends to identify gaps in the market and generate product ideas based on this data.

AI can also be used to **enhance service offerings**. Take the example of customer service: AI-powered chatbots and virtual assistants are increasingly used to provide 24/7 support and personalized customer interactions. These AI systems can learn from past conversations, provide relevant solutions, and even predict customer needs before they arise. By integrating AI into customer service, businesses can enhance their customers' experiences, improve satisfaction, and reduce operational costs.

Furthermore, AI allows businesses to create **customized offerings** that were once impractical. For example, in the fashion industry, AI can be used to offer personalized clothing recommendations based on an individual's preferences, body type, and style history. In the food industry, AI can create personalized meal plans based on a person's dietary preferences and health goals. This level of **personalization** not only drives customer loyalty but also opens new avenues for product and service innovation.

By harnessing the power of AI in product and service development, companies can not only enhance their existing offerings but also create groundbreaking solutions that transform their industries.

AI and Customer Experience: Personalizing Every Interaction

In the modern business landscape, **customer experience** is one of the most important differentiators between companies. AI allows businesses to **personalize customer interactions** in ways that were previously unimaginable, leading to better customer engagement, increased loyalty, and higher sales. By using AI to analyse customer data, businesses can create highly personalized experiences that speak to individual preferences and needs.

One of the most prominent examples of AI-driven customer experience is the use of **personalized marketing**. AI can analyse vast amounts of customer data—such as purchase history, browsing behaviour, and social media activity—to deliver tailored content, product recommendations, and special offers. This not only improves the relevance of marketing messages but also increases the likelihood of conversions, as customers are more likely to engage with content that speaks directly to their interests.

For example, an online retailer can use AI to recommend products to customers based on their previous purchases or even similar products that customers with similar preferences have bought. This type of personalization increases sales and enhances the overall shopping experience. Similarly, AI-powered systems can deliver targeted advertising across digital channels, ensuring that customers see relevant ads based on their browsing history, location, and demographic profile.

In addition to marketing, AI is also revolutionizing **customer service**. AI-powered chatbots and virtual assistants provide customers with quick, personalized responses to their queries. These AI systems can handle a wide range of tasks, from answering frequently asked questions to resolving issues, processing orders, and even offering tailored recommendations. The ability to provide **instant, personalized support** enhances the customer experience and reduces the need for human intervention, leading to faster resolution times and increased customer satisfaction.

For businesses, the power of AI lies in its ability to **predict** customer behaviour and needs before they arise. AI can analyse data to identify trends and anticipate what customers are likely to want next. This predictive capability allows businesses to proactively engage customers with offers and recommendations, improving satisfaction and creating a more seamless experience.

AI-driven personalization and customer experience innovations help businesses build deeper connections with customers, ensuring that their needs are met in real time, and ultimately driving long-term loyalty.

Disrupting Traditional Industries with AI Innovation

One of the most exciting aspects of AI is its ability to **disrupt traditional industries**. As AI continues to evolve, it is transforming industries that have remained relatively unchanged for decades. Businesses that are early adopters of AI can gain a significant competitive advantage by using AI to drive innovation, reduce costs, and create new value propositions.

Take the **automotive industry** as an example. Companies like Tesla have used AI to develop **autonomous vehicles** that challenge the traditional car manufacturing model. By leveraging AI to power self-driving technology, Tesla and other companies are not only revolutionizing the way people drive but also disrupting the entire transportation industry.

Similarly, **fintech** companies are using AI to transform financial services, offering **automated investment advice**, **fraud detection**, and **credit scoring** using machine learning algorithms. Traditional financial institutions that rely on outdated technologies and manual processes risk being left behind as fintech companies use AI to provide faster, more accurate, and more personalized financial services.

In **healthcare**, AI is being used to disrupt traditional diagnostic processes by enabling doctors to **analyse medical images**, **predict disease risk**, and even **develop personalized treatment plans** based on a patient's unique genetic makeup. AI is not just improving the quality of care—it is transforming the very nature of healthcare delivery.

By embracing AI-driven innovation, businesses can not only stay ahead of the curve but also **disrupt entire industries**, creating new market opportunities and fundamentally changing how products and services are delivered.

Future-Proofing Your Business with AI Innovation

As AI continues to evolve and become more sophisticated, businesses must focus on **future-proofing** their operations. The key to long-term success is not just implementing AI but continuously **innovating** and adapting to new developments in AI technology. Businesses that embrace AI-driven innovation are better equipped to **respond to changes** in the market, **adapt to evolving customer preferences**, and **stay ahead of the competition**.

Future-proofing your business involves building a **culture of continuous learning** and **innovation**. AI is rapidly advancing, and organizations must be prepared to incorporate the latest AI developments into their business models. This means investing in research and development, exploring new AI technologies, and creating systems that allow businesses to remain agile and adaptable in an ever-changing landscape.

To stay ahead, businesses must also focus on **ethical AI**. As AI becomes more integrated into everyday life, it is essential to ensure that AI systems are used responsibly and do not perpetuate bias or inequality. By building ethical frameworks into AI initiatives and maintaining transparency with customers about how AI is being used, businesses can ensure they remain trusted leaders in AI-driven innovation.

AI-driven innovation offers businesses an unprecedented opportunity to **transform their operations**, **disrupt industries**, and **gain a competitive edge**. By leveraging AI to rethink business models, enhance product and service offerings, and personalize customer experiences, companies can create groundbreaking solutions that drive growth and sustainability. The businesses that embrace AI innovation today will be the leaders of tomorrow, setting the stage for long-term success in an increasingly AI-driven world.

Chapter 7: Building a Sustainable AI Strategy: Long-Term Success and Continuous Improvement

For AI to continue providing value over the long term, businesses must adopt a **sustainable AI strategy**—one that not only supports current needs but also adapts to future challenges. A sustainable strategy ensures that AI solutions remain relevant, effective, and aligned with the evolving needs of the business and the marketplace. This chapter explores how businesses can build an AI strategy that drives **continuous improvement**, supports **innovation**, and maintains alignment with **long-term organizational goals**.

The Need for Sustainability in AI Strategy

AI is not a one-off project but a long-term investment that requires continual attention, refinement, and scaling. As technology evolves, so too do the capabilities of AI. Models that work well today may not be as effective tomorrow as they are exposed to new data, shifting customer behaviours, and competitive forces. Therefore, businesses must view their AI investments as **dynamic**—not just as a means of solving a single problem but as an ongoing tool for strategic development.

A **sustainable AI strategy** is not simply about **maintaining** AI solutions; it is about **building a system that continuously adapts** and enhances its value over time. Companies must focus on long-term goals and ensure that AI is integrated into the broader business ecosystem, creating synergies across departments and helping to drive the overall success of the organization.

Creating a Culture of Continuous Improvement

At the core of any sustainable AI strategy is a **culture of continuous improvement**. AI technologies evolve, but they need to be constantly optimized and recalibrated to meet new challenges and deliver ongoing value. The foundation of continuous improvement in AI involves establishing **feedback loops** that ensure AI systems are regularly assessed, updated, and refined.

Establishing Feedback Loops

AI models thrive on data, but they can only be as good as the data they are trained on. As new data is collected, AI systems should be **retrained** to account for emerging patterns and behaviours. This ongoing feedback mechanism allows businesses to refine their AI solutions to better address customer needs, adapt to new market conditions, and remain competitive.

For example, an e-commerce business using an AI-powered recommendation engine must constantly update the algorithms based on new purchasing data, customer feedback, and external trends. As the company gathers more data about customer preferences, the AI system becomes more accurate and effective at predicting and recommending products.

To establish feedback loops, businesses need to create a systematic process for evaluating AI systems. This involves:

- **Regular assessments** of AI performance against success metrics.

- **Retraining models** using fresh, relevant data.

- **Monitoring AI's impact** on key business outcomes, such as sales, customer retention, and operational efficiency.

- **Gathering user feedback** on AI interactions to refine models and improve user experience.

By building feedback mechanisms into AI projects, businesses can ensure that their AI systems do not stagnate but continue to evolve in a way that meets the dynamic needs of the business.

Employee Involvement and Engagement

Incorporating AI into daily operations requires engaging employees at every level. AI systems are most effective when those who interact with them can provide valuable feedback, identify potential improvements, and understand the impact of AI on their roles. A culture that encourages employees to **experiment**, **innovate**, and **contribute ideas** will facilitate a stronger connection to the AI solutions in place.

Employee involvement can take several forms:

- **Training and upskilling**: Ensuring employees are well-equipped to work with AI tools is crucial. AI adoption can be a daunting process for those unfamiliar with the technology, so continuous learning opportunities are essential.

- **Cross-functional collaboration**: AI solutions are often applied across multiple departments (sales, marketing, customer service), so creating collaborative environments where employees can share feedback and insights about AI tools will help uncover areas for improvement.

- **Encouraging experimentation**: Employees should feel empowered to experiment with new AI technologies and suggest ways to improve existing models. This fosters an innovative mindset and accelerates the pace of AI adoption and optimization.

Building a culture of continuous improvement requires strong leadership and an open, inclusive environment that encourages **innovation** and **responsiveness**.

Ensuring Ethical AI Governance

AI governance plays a pivotal role in ensuring that AI systems are not only effective but also **ethical**. As AI becomes more integrated into business decision-making processes, its impact on customers, employees, and society at large grows significantly. Organizations must take proactive steps to ensure that AI systems are used responsibly, minimizing harm and ensuring fairness, transparency, and accountability.

Bias and Fairness

One of the most significant ethical challenges in AI is the potential for **bias**. AI models learn from historical data, which may contain inherent biases based on race, gender, age, or other factors. If these biases are not addressed, AI can perpetuate or even amplify discrimination. For example, a recruitment AI system trained on historical hiring data may inadvertently Favor male candidates over female candidates, perpetuating gender disparities in the workplace.

To mitigate this risk, businesses must prioritize **bias detection and removal** throughout the AI development and deployment process. This involves:

- **Diverse data sourcing**: Ensuring that AI models are trained on diverse datasets that reflect a wide range of perspectives and experiences.

- **Bias audits**: Regularly auditing AI systems for potential biases and adjusting where necessary.

- **Transparency in AI decision-making**: Providing clear explanations of how AI models make decisions, which increases accountability and helps businesses identify any unintended consequences of AI usage.

Businesses should also be prepared to **monitor and adjust** their AI systems over time to ensure that they continue to align with ethical standards. As AI models are exposed to new data and use cases, they must remain free from bias and uphold fairness.

Data Privacy and Security

Another essential aspect of AI governance is ensuring the **privacy and security** of customer data. AI systems often rely on large datasets, including personal information, which can present significant privacy risks. Businesses must adhere to **data privacy** regulations such as the **General Data Protection Regulation (GDPR)** and the **California Consumer Privacy Act (CCPA)** to ensure that customer data is handled responsibly.

To achieve this, businesses should implement strict **data protection protocols** to safeguard personal information, such as encryption, anonymization, and access controls. In addition, businesses should establish clear policies regarding **data usage** to ensure transparency and customer trust.

By embedding ethical AI governance into the organization's DNA, businesses can ensure that AI is used in a way that is both effective and responsible, fostering trust among customers and stakeholders.

Aligning AI with Long-Term Business Goals

A sustainable AI strategy must be closely aligned with the broader strategic goals of the organization. AI initiatives should not be siloed or disconnected from the company's mission and vision. Instead, AI should be an integral part of the strategic framework, supporting long-term goals such as customer satisfaction, innovation, and profitability.

Strategic Alignment

For AI to create long-term value, it must support key **business objectives**. This means that AI should be deployed in areas that have the highest potential for business impact. For example, if a company's goal is to enhance **customer experience**, AI could be applied to customer service via chatbots, personalized recommendations, or predictive analytics. If a company aims to increase **efficiency**, AI can automate repetitive tasks and optimize internal processes.

AI's alignment with business goals is a dynamic process. As businesses evolve, so do their goals and needs. Therefore, businesses must regularly **review and adjust** their AI strategy to ensure it continues to support long-term objectives. This requires close collaboration between business leaders, data scientists, and other key stakeholders to ensure that AI is deployed where it can generate the most significant value.

Building Scalability into AI Projects

AI scalability is a crucial consideration for ensuring the long-term sustainability of AI initiatives. As businesses grow and AI solutions are expanded, it's essential to **build systems** and processes that can scale to accommodate increased demand, larger data sets, and more complex algorithms.

A scalable AI infrastructure involves:

- **Cloud-based solutions**: Leveraging cloud computing platforms for scalable storage, processing power, and data analytics.

- **Modular AI models**: Designing AI systems that can be easily adjusted, expanded, or replaced as business needs evolve.

- **Agile methodologies**: Employing agile development practices that allow for quick iterations, adjustments, and scaling.

Investing in scalable AI infrastructure early on will allow businesses to avoid the pitfalls of poorly planned AI systems that fail to scale as the organization grows.

Leveraging AI for Innovation and Market Leadership

In addition to supporting operational efficiency, AI can be a powerful tool for **driving innovation** and maintaining **market leadership**. AI technologies can help businesses stay ahead of competitors by uncovering **new insights**, **improving product development**, and **creating differentiated offerings**. AI allows businesses to innovate faster, respond to market shifts, and anticipate customer needs.

Innovation through AI

Businesses can leverage AI to drive product and service innovation by identifying gaps in the market and creating solutions that meet new customer needs. AI can be used to analyse customer feedback, market trends, and competitor offerings to inform the development of new products or services.

For example, AI can be used to **analyse social media trends** and uncover emerging consumer behaviours. By using this data, businesses can **create new products**, tailor existing offerings, and refine marketing strategies to stay ahead of competitors.

AI as a Competitive Advantage

To remain competitive, businesses must leverage AI to create unique value propositions that cannot easily be replicated by competitors. AI can help businesses identify **niche markets**, improve **customer targeting**, and provide **personalized** experiences that differentiate their offerings.

By investing in AI-driven innovation and continuously improving AI systems, businesses can establish themselves as **leaders** in their industries, creating a sustainable competitive advantage that ensures long-term success.

Measuring AI Success: KPIs and Performance Metrics

To ensure the sustainability of AI strategies, businesses must define clear **Key Performance Indicators (KPIs)** and regularly measure the impact of AI on business outcomes. These KPIs will vary depending on the goals of each AI initiative but should always be tied to tangible business objectives.

Common KPIs for AI initiatives include:

- **Operational efficiency**: Metrics like cost savings, time reductions, and process optimization.

- **Customer satisfaction**: NPS scores, customer retention rates, and overall customer engagement.

- **Revenue growth**: Increases in sales, upsell success, or new revenue streams generated by AI-driven solutions.

- **Employee productivity**: The impact of AI on employee roles, including reductions in mundane tasks and increases in value-added activities.

By establishing clear KPIs and regularly tracking performance, businesses can ensure that AI continues to deliver value and adjust as needed to maximize impact.

Building a Long-Term AI Roadmap

To succeed with AI, businesses need to develop a long-term AI **roadmap** that outlines the key milestones, resources, and timelines for AI adoption and scaling. This roadmap should be flexible enough to accommodate changes in the market, technology, and business goals while providing a clear path forward for the organization.

A long-term AI roadmap should include:

- **Short- and long-term goals**: Setting clear objectives for immediate AI initiatives and longer-term ambitions.

- **Resources and investment**: Identifying the resources needed to support AI initiatives, including data infrastructure, AI tools, and talent.

- **Timeline for implementation**: Creating a timeline that outlines key milestones, from initial AI pilots to full-scale deployment.

By developing a clear roadmap, businesses can ensure that AI becomes a **strategic asset** that drives sustainable growth and innovation for years to come.

In conclusion, building a sustainable AI strategy requires **continuous improvement**, strong governance, alignment with long-term business goals, and a focus on innovation. AI must be seen as a **dynamic tool** that evolves alongside the organization and adapts to changing market conditions. By fostering a culture of innovation, ensuring scalability, and focusing on ethical use, businesses can harness the full potential of AI and create lasting competitive advantages in the marketplace.

Chapter 8: Staying Ahead in a Rapidly Evolving Landscape with Generative AI and Large Language Models

While much of the focus in recent years has been on AI applications like machine learning and computer vision, the future of AI is increasingly dominated by **Generative AI (GenAI) and Large Language Models (LLMs)**—two emerging technologies that are poised to transform businesses across sectors.

Generative AI, which includes tools capable of creating new content such as text, images, and even code, is pushing the boundaries of innovation. LLMs, such as OpenAI's GPT models, have revolutionized natural language processing (NLP), making it possible for machines to understand, generate, and interact with human language in highly sophisticated ways. These technologies offer businesses new opportunities for automation, content creation, decision-making, and customer engagement.

This chapter will explore the **future of AI**, focusing on the emerging trends of **Generative AI** and **LLMs** and their potential impact on industries. We will discuss how businesses can leverage these cutting-edge technologies, stay ahead of the competition, and create long-term value through AI-driven innovation.

The Rise of Generative AI: Transforming Creativity and Content Production

Generative AI is rapidly gaining traction as one of the most exciting areas of AI development. Unlike traditional AI, which typically works to analyse or classify existing data, Generative AI can create entirely new data—whether that be text, images, videos, music, or code. This ability to **generate content** opens a wide range of possibilities for businesses, particularly in areas such as **marketing**, **customer service**, **product design**, and **personalized experiences**.

Content Creation and Personalization at Scale

One of the most transformative applications of Generative AI is in content creation. Traditionally, businesses have relied on human teams to generate marketing materials, product descriptions, and other content. With tools like **GPT-3** and other advanced models, businesses can now automatically generate high-quality written content, including blog posts, ad copy, product descriptions, social media content, and more. These AI systems can produce content that mimics human language patterns, making it almost indistinguishable from content created by humans.

Generative AI also enables businesses to deliver **personalized content** to customers at scale. For example, an e-commerce company could use Generative AI to tailor product recommendations, personalized email campaigns, and even chatbots that communicate in a style consistent with the customer's preferences. By leveraging these AI tools, businesses can provide **hyper-personalized experiences** that engage customers more deeply and drive higher conversion rates.

Moreover, in industries like **entertainment** and **gaming**, Generative AI is revolutionizing content production. AI models are being used to **create artwork**, **generate 3D models**, and even **write scripts** for video games and films. These tools can help studios reduce production costs and accelerate the content creation process, enabling the rapid generation of high-quality media that was once time-consuming and resource intensive.

Improving Product Development with AI-Generated Prototypes

Generative AI is also transforming **product design** and development. Traditionally, creating product prototypes is a time-consuming process that involves collaboration between designers, engineers, and product managers. With Generative AI, businesses can automate aspects of product development by generating **AI-driven prototypes** based on specific inputs, such as functional requirements, material constraints, and aesthetic preferences.

For example, in the **fashion industry**, Generative AI can be used to generate clothing designs based on trends, customer preferences, and historical sales data. Similarly, in **automotive** or **industrial design**, AI tools can suggest new product designs or manufacturing processes that improve efficiency and reduce costs. These innovations not only enhance creativity but also streamline development cycles, enabling businesses to bring new products to market more quickly and with greater precision.

Large Language Models (LLMs): Revolutionizing Communication and Decision-Making

While Generative AI is rapidly advancing, **Large Language Models (LLMs)** such as OpenAI's GPT-4, Google's PaLM, and Anthropic's Claude are at the forefront of transforming how machines interact with human language. LLMs have revolutionized **natural language processing (NLP)** by enabling machines to understand, generate, and respond to text in ways that are more context-aware and sophisticated than ever before.

Enhancing Customer Support and Engagement

One of the most promising applications of LLMs is in **customer service**. Chatbots and virtual assistants powered by LLMs can understand a wide range of customer queries and respond with relevant, contextually appropriate information. These systems are capable of handling complex interactions that would typically require human agents, such as troubleshooting issues, answering detailed questions, and providing tailored recommendations.

Unlike earlier AI chatbots, which relied on rigid scripts and rule-based responses, LLM-powered chatbots can **carry on nuanced conversations**, manage multiple topics, and even recognize **sentiment** in customer interactions. This allows businesses to offer **24/7 support** with high-quality responses, significantly reducing operational costs while maintaining a high level of customer satisfaction.

In industries like **banking**, **telecommunications**, and **e-commerce**, where customer inquiries can be highly variable, LLMs have proven to be a game changer in delivering **fast, accurate**, and **personalized customer support** at scale.

AI-Enhanced Decision-Making

LLMs also provide significant advantages in **business intelligence** and **decision-making**. By processing vast amounts of data and extracting meaningful insights, these models can help businesses make more informed decisions. LLMs can be used to **analyse market trends**, **predict customer behaviour**, and **automatically generate reports** based on complex datasets.

For example, in the **financial services** industry, LLMs can help analysts by summarizing market reports, identifying key financial trends, and even generating predictive models to guide investment decisions. In **marketing**, businesses can use LLMs to analyse customer feedback, surveys, and social media posts to identify sentiment and improve campaign strategies.

The power of LLMs in decision-making lies in their ability to quickly process and synthesize vast amounts of unstructured text data, providing executives and managers with **actionable insights** that would have taken much longer to uncover using traditional methods.

AI-Powered Automation: A Key to Future Business Success

As AI continues to advance, the potential for **AI-driven automation** will increase significantly. Automation powered by AI and LLMs will extend beyond simple task automation to include more complex, **strategic decision-making** and **creative processes**.

Automating Business Processes

Businesses are already using AI and automation tools to handle repetitive tasks such as data entry, invoicing, scheduling, and customer outreach. With the rise of **Generative AI**, however, automation can be expanded to more advanced tasks, such as content generation, coding, design, and even business strategy formulation. This ability to automate creative and strategic processes will free up human employees to focus on higher-value tasks, while also ensuring that key processes remain efficient, consistent, and scalable.

For example, AI tools are already being used in marketing automation to create customized ads, generate social media posts, and even develop email campaigns based on customer data. In the field of software development, AI-powered tools can assist with **code generation** and **bug fixing**, improving productivity and reducing the time it takes to develop applications.

Improved Business Intelligence

AI-powered automation tools, such as those based on LLMs, can process and analyse data at scale, transforming how organizations interact with their data. Businesses can leverage AI to **automate data analysis**, summarize insights, and generate reports in real-time, allowing them to make data-driven decisions more quickly and effectively.

For example, AI can automate the generation of financial reports, sales forecasts, and performance analytics, enabling decision-makers to focus on interpreting the insights rather than spending time gathering and processing data. This level of automation will revolutionize industries where timely decision-making is crucial, such as finance, retail, and healthcare.

The Ethical Implications of Generative AI and LLMs

As businesses embrace Generative AI and LLMs, ethical considerations will play a crucial role in their responsible deployment. These technologies can provide businesses with unprecedented capabilities, but they also raise important questions about **bias**, **privacy**, and **accountability**.

Ensuring Fairness and Transparency

Generative AI models and LLMs are only as unbiased as the data they are trained on. If these models are trained on biased data, they can perpetuate harmful stereotypes or produce unfair outcomes, especially in areas like hiring, lending, or customer interactions.

To mitigate these risks, businesses must prioritize fairness in the development and deployment of AI systems. This involves ensuring that data is diverse, inclusive, and free from biases that could lead to discrimination.

In addition, transparency in AI decision-making is essential. As AI becomes more involved in business processes, companies must ensure that AI models are **explainable** and **accountable**. This allows stakeholders to understand how AI arrived at its conclusions and ensures that businesses are held accountable for their AI-driven decisions.

Data Privacy and Security

Given that Generative AI and LLMs often require large datasets to train, businesses must be vigilant about how customer data is collected, stored, and processed. Ensuring compliance with data privacy regulations such as **GDPR** and **CCPA** is crucial to building trust with customers. Businesses must also establish robust data security measures to protect against potential breaches and misuse of sensitive information.

Preparing for the Future: Building an AI-Ready Organization

To stay ahead of the curve and leverage the full potential of Generative AI and LLMs, businesses must build an **AI-ready organization**. This involves:

1. **Investing in AI talent**: Organizations need to hire or train data scientists, engineers, and AI experts who can develop, maintain, and optimize Generative AI and LLM systems.

2. **Fostering a culture of innovation**: Encourage employees to think creatively and experiment with AI tools, allowing them to identify new opportunities for AI to drive value.

3. **Scalable infrastructure**: Businesses must ensure that they have the technological infrastructure to support the growing demands of AI, such as cloud-based platforms for storage, processing power, and model training.

4. **Ongoing monitoring and optimization**: Continuously evaluate AI models to ensure they are delivering the intended outcomes and adjust based on real-time feedback and changing business needs.

Leading the AI Revolution

Generative AI and Large Language Models represent the cutting edge of AI innovation, offering businesses the tools to transform their operations, enhance customer engagement, and drive new levels of creativity. As AI continues to evolve, organizations that embrace these technologies will be well-positioned to lead their industries, disrupt traditional models, and unlock new growth opportunities.

By understanding the potential of GenAI and LLMs, staying ahead of emerging trends, and investing in ethical, scalable AI solutions, businesses can harness the full power of AI to innovate, grow, and thrive in the future. The next phase of AI is not just about adopting new technologies—it's about **transforming the way businesses think, operate, and engage with their customers**. Embrace the future of AI and position your organization as a leader in the AI-driven world.

Chapter 9: Implementing AI Across Business Functions: Practical Roadmap for Success

While the potential of AI is vast, its successful integration requires a well-thought-out approach that aligns with organizational goals and addresses specific business needs. AI should not be seen as a one-size-fits-all tool; rather, it should be tailored to enhance each function of the business in a way that drives tangible outcomes.

This chapter will provide a comprehensive **roadmap for implementing AI** across business functions, detailing how AI can be applied in **marketing**, **sales**, **operations**, **customer service**, **human resources**, and **finance**. We will explore practical steps for integrating AI into each department, the challenges businesses may face, and the strategies for overcoming these challenges. By the end of this chapter, businesses will have a clear understanding of how to deploy AI solutions strategically across their organization, ensuring that AI delivers measurable value in every area.

1. AI in Marketing: Personalization and Predictive Analytics

Marketing is one of the most fertile grounds for AI implementation. With consumers increasingly expecting personalized experiences, businesses must harness AI to deliver tailored content, optimize customer journeys, and predict future buying behaviour. AI-powered tools, such as **predictive analytics** and **customer segmentation algorithms**, can help marketers make data-driven decisions and deliver highly targeted campaigns.

Step 1: Implement AI-Powered Personalization

AI enables businesses to **personalize customer interactions** in real-time. By analysing customer data, such as browsing history, purchase behaviour, and social media interactions, AI can predict individual preferences and suggest products or services accordingly. AI-driven tools such as **recommendation engines** have already transformed e-commerce platforms like Amazon and Netflix by suggesting products or media tailored to users' tastes.

To implement AI-powered personalization in marketing, businesses should:

- Use **machine learning** to segment customers based on demographic data and behavioural patterns.

- Deploy **AI-based recommendation systems** to provide personalized product suggestions, offers, or content.

- Integrate **NLP** (natural language processing) into email marketing and customer interactions to create personalized messaging.

Step 2: Predict Customer Behaviour with AI

Predictive analytics is another key application of AI in marketing. By analysing historical data, AI models can predict **future trends**, **customer preferences**, and **churn risks**. Predictive models can also optimize marketing campaigns by identifying the best times to engage with customers, the most effective channels for outreach, and the content that is most likely to drive conversions.

To leverage AI for predictive analytics, businesses should:

- **Analyse past purchasing data** to predict future sales trends.

- Use **sentiment analysis** to measure customer satisfaction and predict the likelihood of customer retention or churn.

- Implement **AI-driven campaign optimization tools** that automatically adjust bids and budgets based on predicted customer behaviour.

By using AI for predictive marketing, businesses can optimize their marketing efforts, improve customer engagement, and increase revenue.

2. AI in Sales: Lead Scoring and Automation

Sales teams are under constant pressure to find high-quality leads, close deals, and meet targets. AI can help by automating repetitive tasks, predicting which leads are most likely to convert, and providing insights to guide sales strategies. AI-powered tools such as **sales forecasting** and **lead scoring algorithms** can help businesses close deals faster and more efficiently.

Step 1: Automate Lead Scoring

AI can significantly improve **lead scoring** by analysing historical customer interactions and identifying patterns that indicate a high likelihood of conversion. Machine learning algorithms can evaluate leads based on factors such as **engagement level**, **demographics**, and **previous buying behaviour** to automatically score and prioritize them for sales teams.

To integrate AI into lead scoring, businesses should:

- Use **machine learning** models to predict which leads are most likely to close.

- Implement **AI-based CRM systems** that automatically update lead scores based on customer interactions, allowing sales teams to focus on the most promising prospects.

- Automate the process of **nurturing leads** through personalized email campaigns and follow-ups generated by AI systems.

Step 2: Implement AI-Driven Sales Forecasting

Sales forecasting is another area where AI can add significant value. By analysing historical sales data, customer behaviour, and market trends, AI models can generate more accurate forecasts, enabling sales teams to better allocate resources and set realistic targets.

To implement AI-driven sales forecasting, businesses should:

- Use AI models to identify **seasonal trends** and **market conditions** that may impact sales.

- Integrate AI-powered forecasting tools into the **CRM system** to continuously update predictions based on real-time data.

- Leverage **AI-powered chatbots** to interact with leads and gather insights that inform sales strategies.

By automating lead scoring and improving sales forecasting, businesses can close deals more effectively, optimize their sales pipeline, and drive revenue growth.

3. AI in Operations: Process Optimization and Automation

In operations, AI can be used to optimize everything from supply chain management to inventory control, improving efficiency and reducing costs. AI-driven automation in operations can streamline processes, reduce human error, and allow businesses to focus on strategic decision-making.

Step 1: Optimize Supply Chain Management with AI

AI can help businesses optimize their **supply chain** by predicting demand, managing inventory levels, and optimizing delivery routes. AI models can analyse historical sales data and external factors, such as weather or market conditions, to forecast demand with high accuracy. This allows businesses to adjust their supply chain in real-time, ensuring they can meet customer demand without overstocking or understocking products.

To implement AI in supply chain management, businesses should:

- Use **predictive analytics** to forecast demand and adjust production schedules accordingly.

- Implement **AI-powered inventory management systems** that automatically reorder products based on current stock levels and anticipated demand.

- Integrate **AI-driven logistics systems** to optimize delivery routes and reduce shipping costs.

Step 2: Automate Routine Operational Tasks

AI can also automate repetitive and mundane operational tasks such as **data entry**, **report generation**, and **scheduling**. By automating these processes, businesses can reduce human error and free up employees to focus on more strategic initiatives.

To integrate AI into operations, businesses should:

- Use **AI bots** to automate routine tasks such as data processing and report generation.

- Implement **robotic process automation (RPA)** tools to automate repetitive workflows and streamline back-office operations.

- Leverage **AI-driven scheduling tools** to optimize workforce allocation and resource planning.

By optimizing supply chains and automating routine tasks, AI can drive significant cost savings and efficiency improvements across business operations.

4. AI in Customer Service: Chatbots and Sentiment Analysis

Customer service is another area where AI is making significant strides. AI-powered **chatbots** and **virtual assistants** can handle customer inquiries, troubleshoot issues, and provide personalized support at scale. Additionally, AI can analyse customer sentiment to improve service quality and identify areas for improvement.

Step 1: Implement AI-Powered Chatbots

AI chatbots can interact with customers in real-time, providing instant responses to frequently asked questions, processing orders, and troubleshooting basic issues. With advanced natural language processing (NLP) capabilities, these chatbots can hold meaningful conversations and provide relevant responses based on context.

To implement AI-powered chatbots, businesses should:

- Deploy **AI-driven chatbot platforms** that can integrate with websites, mobile apps, and social media.

- Use **machine learning algorithms** to continuously improve chatbot responses based on customer feedback and interactions.

- Automate basic customer service tasks, such as order tracking and appointment scheduling, to reduce wait times and improve customer satisfaction.

Step 2: Use AI for Sentiment Analysis

AI can also be used to analyse customer sentiment through **sentiment analysis** tools, which evaluate text data from customer reviews, social media posts, and support tickets. By understanding how customers feel about a product or service, businesses can make proactive improvements and enhance customer experience.

To integrate sentiment analysis, businesses should:

- Use **AI-powered text analytics tools** to analyse customer feedback and identify common issues or pain points.

- Implement **real-time sentiment tracking** across social media platforms and customer reviews to gauge public opinion.

- Leverage AI insights to **improve customer support** and personalize interactions based on customer sentiment.

By integrating AI into customer service, businesses can provide **24/7 support**, improve **response times**, and enhance the overall customer experience.

5. AI in Human Resources: Recruitment and Employee Engagement

Human resources (HR) are another area where AI is having a profound impact. AI tools can help businesses **automate recruitment**, **improve employee engagement**, and **predict turnover**. By leveraging AI, HR departments can streamline their processes and make more data-driven decisions.

Step 1: Automate Recruitment with AI

AI can automate the recruitment process by screening resumes, ranking candidates, and even conducting initial interviews. Machine learning algorithms can be used to identify the most qualified candidates based on their skills, experience, and potential cultural fit.

To implement AI in recruitment, businesses should:

- Use **AI-powered recruitment platforms** that automate resume screening and initial candidate assessments.

- Implement **AI-driven chatbots** to conduct pre-screening interviews and answer candidate queries.

- Leverage **predictive analytics** to assess the likelihood of a candidate's long-term success within the organization.

Step 2: Predict Employee Turnover and Engagement

AI can help businesses predict **employee turnover** and identify strategies to improve **employee engagement**. By analysing historical data and employee behaviour, AI models can identify early warning signs of disengagement, allowing HR teams to take proactive measures to retain talent.

To integrate AI for employee engagement, businesses should:

- Use **predictive analytics** to forecast employee turnover based on factors such as job satisfaction, performance reviews, and career development.

- Implement **AI-based engagement surveys** to collect real-time feedback from employees and identify areas for improvement.

- Leverage **AI-powered coaching tools** to help employees develop their skills and achieve their career goals.

By using AI to optimize recruitment and employee engagement, businesses can build a more productive and satisfied workforce.

AI as a Strategic Business Driver

The implementation of AI across business functions can significantly enhance productivity, drive innovation, and improve customer satisfaction. By applying AI strategically in **marketing**, **sales**, **operations**, **customer service**, **human resources**, and other departments, businesses can streamline processes, automate routine tasks, and unlock new opportunities for growth.

By following the practical roadmap outlined in this chapter, businesses can harness the full potential of AI and position themselves for long-term success in an increasingly competitive and AI-driven world.

Conclusion: The Path Forward in AI Adoption and Scaling

As we conclude this exploration of AI implementation and scaling, **AI is not just a passing trend**; it is the backbone of a new wave of innovation that has the power to transform businesses across every industry. The journey to scale AI, however, is not a one-time event—it is a continuous process that requires planning, execution, and, most importantly, adaptability. For businesses to harness the full potential of AI, they must embrace it not only as a tool for automation and efficiency but as a catalyst for innovation and long-term success.

Throughout this book, we have explored the **foundations of AI implementation**, the **challenges and obstacles** businesses face, and the **strategies for scaling AI** to achieve measurable, sustainable outcomes. We have seen how AI can be integrated across various business functions—**from marketing and sales to operations, HR, and finance**—to unlock new growth opportunities, streamline operations, and provide better customer experiences.

The Strategic Importance of AI Adoption

At the core of any AI implementation strategy is the alignment with **business goals**. AI, when properly aligned, acts as a **powerful enabler** that can drive business transformation. By focusing on the right business objectives, whether it's increasing operational efficiency, enhancing personalization, or optimizing customer service, AI can serve as a foundational driver for growth.

But this transformation is not merely about technology; it is about creating a new way of thinking about business processes and aligning AI with the **core values and mission** of the organization.

Embracing a Culture of Innovation and Collaboration

Scaling AI successfully requires more than just adopting the latest tools; it requires **cultivating a culture** that encourages **continuous learning**, **experimentation**, and **cross-functional collaboration**. AI should be embedded in every aspect of the business, from decision-making processes to customer-facing interactions. Leaders must prioritize **employee education** and **upskilling**, ensuring that teams across the organization are equipped to leverage AI to their advantage.

The most successful AI-powered organizations will be those that embrace **collaborative innovation**—where technical teams and business leaders work together to create solutions that solve real-world problems. **Agility** and **openness to change** will be key attributes of businesses that thrive in an AI-driven future.

Overcoming Challenges and Navigating Ethical Concerns

While AI holds immense promise, the path forward is not without its challenges. **Data quality**, **integration**, **bias**, and **ethical considerations** are significant hurdles that must be addressed in any AI strategy. Businesses must create **governance structures**, ensure transparency, and remain accountable to both customers and employees as they adopt AI technologies.

Ethical AI will be a cornerstone of AI adoption in the years to come. As AI systems become increasingly responsible for decision-making, businesses must ensure that these decisions are made with fairness, inclusivity, and transparency at the forefront. By addressing these challenges head-on, businesses can foster trust with customers, employees, and regulators alike.

The Future of AI: An Ongoing Evolution

The journey of AI adoption does not end with its initial implementation. It is a continual process of **optimization**, **feedback**, and **growth**. The **advancements in AI technologies**— from **Generative AI** and **Large Language Models (LLMs)** to **reinforcement learning** and **AI-driven automation**—will continue to evolve at a rapid pace, offering businesses new opportunities to innovate and stay competitive. Businesses must remain **agile** and **future-focused**, constantly refining their AI strategies to align with technological advancements and shifting market conditions.

The future of AI lies not just in implementing it to solve existing problems, but in using it to unlock new **business models**, create **new revenue streams**, and build **personalized customer experiences** that were once unimaginable. As AI continues to mature, businesses that prioritize **innovation**, **responsibility**, and **scalability** will be best positioned to lead in their respective industries.

Final Thoughts: Leading the AI-Driven Transformation

AI is not merely a technology—it is a **transformational force** that is reshaping industries, business models, and customer expectations. Whether you are just beginning your AI journey or are looking to scale AI across your organization, the key to success lies in **strategic vision**, **collaboration**, and **ethical responsibility**. The businesses that succeed will be those that treat AI as an enabler of growth, to continuously innovate, and as a catalyst for lasting, positive change.

As AI continues to evolve, businesses must be willing to embrace it, learn from it, and adapt to its growing influence. By doing so, they can not only achieve their current goals but also unlock new opportunities for **long-term success**, becoming leaders in a world where AI is the backbone of business transformation.

The future is AI-driven—and the path to success is just beginning.

Acknowledgement

I would like to take a moment to express my heartfelt gratitude to those who have supported me throughout this journey. A special thank you goes to my beloved wife, Maryam. Your unconditional support and love have been my guiding light through every difficulty and challenge. You have stood by me with unwavering strength and encouragement, believing in me even when I struggled to believe in myself. Your patience and understanding have made this journey possible, and I am endlessly grateful to have you by my side. Thank you for inspiring me every day and for being my partner in life and in dreams.

With all my love, Hamid

About The Author

My name is Hamid Oudi, and my life has been shaped by experiences of change, growth, and a desire to make meaningful contributions. I was born in Iran and moved to the United Kingdom in 2006 as a child. Adjusting to a new country with a different language and culture was a significant challenge, but it also taught me resilience, adaptability, and the value of curiosity.

These experiences inspired me to write *The Curious Journey of Biscuit Boy*. It's a simple, heartfelt story about transformation and finding one's place in the world—something I've experienced in my own journey. The story follows Biscuit Boy, a chocolate treat that comes to life, as he learns to navigate the world and discover his purpose. Writing this book allowed me to reflect on the lessons I've learned and share them in a way that's relatable and meaningful.

Professionally, I've always been drawn to technology and problem-solving. With a background in engineering and data science, I've spent my career exploring ways to use technology to make life easier and more efficient. As the director of MyFalcon Limited, I focus on designing systems that help businesses make better decisions using data and AI. My work has always been about finding practical solutions to real-world problems, and I'm grateful for the opportunities I've had to contribute to this field.

Sharing knowledge has also been an important part of my journey. I enjoy breaking down complex ideas and making them accessible, whether through my YouTube channel or conversations with others. Technology, to me, is a tool for empowerment, and I'm passionate about helping people and organizations use it to create positive change.

Looking back, I see my journey as one of gradual growth and learning. Moving to a new country taught me resilience and adaptability, while my work and writing have allowed me to contribute in small but meaningful ways. I still have much to learn and do, but I'm grateful for the path I've taken and excited for what lies ahead.

YouTube Channel at:

@myfalconuk

Printed in Great Britain
by Amazon

59277627R00056